Income and Expense Tracker for Authors

A Guide to Effortless Bookkeeping, Optimized Taxes, and Reduced Tax-Prep Expenses

Ashley Guion, CPA, MSA

Why should you listen to me?

- **I'm a CPA with years of public accounting experience**

- I've worked with hundreds of small business owners to better understand their financial situation

- From those experiences (and my education), I know what tax preparers are looking for at tax-filing time. **This book, should you choose to fill it out, will save you money in tax prep.**
    - If your preparer charges $150/hr and the results of completing this workbook saves them four hours of tax prep time… **That's $600 you saved** just by improving your record keeping (minus the cost of this awesome organizer, of course)
    - Sure, tax prep fees are usually deductible, *but do you really want that expense*? Wouldn't you rather have that course you've been eye-balling? Or that really awesome cover?

- The tax-prep savings alone aren't the only reason though. You're a business owner now. An author. **This is a job** (or maybe a really expensive hobby… I don't get into hobby loss/income here but I do in my handbook)

- **If you're doing this as a business…act like it**. Take the steps that will legitimize it. The money and stress you will save yourself by staying more on track of your finances…trust me, **it's worth it.**
    - Actually, using something like QuickBooks Online is *my favorite*, but that's for when you can afford the monthly subscription fee. I could totally geek out on you right now on all the benefits of using something like QBO to track and organize everything but I won't want to scare you off *quite* yet.

- I used my experience not only as a CPA but as an author to craft this workbook and make it as relevant as possible. **There are tips and tricks throughout.** Use what you want and ditch the rest.

Disclosure & Copyright

My lawyer makes me say it…

- **I'm an accountant, but not your accountant.** Please contact a local professional that is knowledgeable about your specific situation (especially if you're not US based). The content is for informational and discussion purposes and is all my opinion and therefore should not be considered as tax, legal, or financial advice.
- I know you probably hate to hear that, but the content in this book will be as generic as possible. I don't want someone to come back and say "well, you said I could deduct XYZ." This is a broad-strokes workbook that will educate you in a way that makes you not want to vomit or break out in hives. It is not your guide to absolutes (especially because tax laws change every year)
- I'll drop specifics where I can, but recognize that everyone's situation is different, that's why CPAs are paid the big bucks for customized advice and we why we bill out in six minute increments.

Second edition updates: No longer year-specific, shows 2024's Form 8829

Cover designed by Get Covers

Interior images by FreePik, Pexels, and Pixabay

ISBN: 978-1-956865-51-6 (paperback)

Published by Libra Libros LLC

How To Use

Yellow highlighted sheets can be used for direct tax prep - taking the guesswork out of it

- This is not a substitute for working with personalized accountant, but will put you on the right path for your business
- I'll sprinkle tidbits of advice and experience throughout the book to give you manageable pieces of content as well as providing you with as many resources that seem useful in the context of our mission here – which is to give you financial control and insight over your company!
- These pages are available for pdf purchase in case you wanted/needed to print them out and hole-punch them to organize them how it works best for you (and recycle any unwanted pages)
- I created this as if you were my client and I'm discussing business strategy with you.
    - **Using this book will prepare you for a great year where you can finally understand your numbers**
- We'll even end on some tax forms/guides that will make tax prep less expensive/painful
    - **Pro tip: Time is money - don't make your CPA add up your receipts for you :-)**
        - Or, if you're doing it yourself, don't do that to future you. Make it easy on yourself by doing some guided monthly maintenance
- **Use what you need, ignore what you don't. Do what's best for you.**
- Feel free to drop any yearly deadlines (book launches, recurrent annual expenses, book signings, vacations, promos, deadlines, etc) on the yearly and monthly calendars. And also feel free to highlight the big wins on there. Maybe when you pull this book out in five years and you look at that calendar the Nostalgia Monster will grab hold and you'll realize how far you've come.

Contents

Writing/Book Publishing Goals

What are your one-year goals?

What are your five-year goals?

What are your ten-year goals?

What are your twenty-year goals?

Reiterate Your WHY

When you're having a hard time putting your butt in the chair and doing the work, I want you to remember this string of questions:

Why are you doing this?

Who are you writing for?

What is your end goal?

Do you have a financial goal in mind? Or is it a soft goal?

WIPs (Works in Progress)

Any big projects that you're working on this year

Check those puppies off as you get 'em done

(Cue Toby Keith's *My List*)

- ☐
- ☐
- ☐
- ☐
- ☐
- ☐
- ☐
- ☐
- ☐
- ☐
- ☐
- ☐
- ☐
- ☐
- ☐
- ☐

Author Wishlist

Add any writing resources that you want to invest in

(Remember, they're deductible when you buy them!)

- ☐
- ☐
- ☐
- ☐
- ☐
- ☐
- ☐
- ☐
- ☐
- ☐
- ☐
- ☐
- ☐
- ☐
- ☐
- ☐

Revenue

At month-end, calculate the total revenue for each month and use it to populate the monthly summary pages.

At year-end, add up all of the monthly summaries and populate the yearly total pages.

Revenue Reporting

- **Income is income**
  - "I only need to start claiming it when XYZ"
    - Don't play that game
    - Start reporting when you earn it - be honest
- We authors have lots of different sources of revenue throughout the year
  - Royalties from our books, Audiobooks, Patreon, Vella, direct sales, in-person sales, Substack, editing, beta reading, cover-designing, PA-ing, etc.
  - It's all related and therefore, I believe, it can be reported together on the same schedule on your tax return.
- Assuming you're a cash basis reporter - most are - track all of your revenue (income) received
  - For example, even if you earned $500 from Amazon royalties in December, you aren't actually PAID those royalties until the following year - therefore, you **<u>don't</u>** include those here. Look at your bank <u>deposits</u> or your actual payment print outs to confirm payments
    - **<u>Now's the time I tell you to open a separate business checking account, Square, PayPal, etc</u>**
  - You may get 1099s from various sources for the income YOU received. Keep those in your records

Expenses

At month-end, calculate the total expenses for each category for that month and use those totals to populate the monthly summary pages.

At year-end, add up all of the monthly summaries and populate the yearly total pages.

Expenses

- If you're cash basis - you take the deduction **when the cash was paid** (or credit card was swiped).
- We authors have lots of different sources of expenses throughout the year
    - Covers, Editors, Audiobook production, Classes, Workbooks (like this one), Recurring charges for websites/domains/plugins, advertising/marketing, etc
- **If you want to save money on your taxes, have the expense categories organized correctly, and subtotal them for your accountant**
    - Note: usually they don't want to see the invoices unless it's something out-of-place - just give them totals usually
- Current De Minimis Threshold per the IRS - $2,500
    - Anything less than $2,500 can be recorded in an expense category in the trackers.
    - **Anything over $2,500 - make sure you mention to your accountant so they (or you) can capitalize and depreciate it on your fixed asset schedule if necessary (Form 4562).**
- Remember, keep track of your vendors and get copies of their W9s so you can issue them 1099s if necessary
    - The penalties are rough if you don't do this

Expense Categories

Assuming a Schedule C Tax Return (single-member LLC or sole-proprietor)

(Though, the categories will *mostly* work for other entities as well)

- **Advertising**
  - Costs for promoting the business
  - Advertising costs (online ads, book promotions)
    - Facebook ads, amazon ads, TikTok ads, etc
  - Website maintenance and hosting fees
  - Book launch event expenses
  - Website
  - Some charitable donations may qualify - ask your preparer

- **Car and Truck Expenses**
  - Vehicle-related expenses for business use
  - You'll probably just track mileage…
    - *In the workbook tracker so don't double count it twice by including expenses here as well*

- **Commissions**
  - Agent commissions

Expense Categories

Remember, this is not an exhaustive list and it's currently how ***I*** view what should go in the various buckets

- **Contract Labor**
  - Payments to contractors or freelancers.
  - Royalty payments to co-authors or contributors
  - Make sure you're issuing 1099s as appropriate
    - $600 threshold for services; $10 threshold for royalties

- **Depreciation and Section 179 Expense Deduction**
  - Depreciation of business assets
  - *Usually calculated by your accountant*

- **Employee Benefits Program**
  - Costs for employee benefit programs
  - Employee health insurance

- **Insurance**
  - *Business* insurance premiums (not health or life)
  - Professional liability insurance

Expense Categories

- **Interest**
  - Interest on business loans or credit cards.
  - Not your home mortgage int or student loan interest

- **Legal and Professional Services**
  - Legal or accounting fees for the business
  - Legal advice or fees related to contracts or intellectual property rights
  - CPA or tax preparation fees
  - Payroll processing fees

- **Office Expenses**
  - Supplies and expenses related to the business office
  - Stationery and Supplies
    - Pens, pencils, notebooks, notepads, paper, envelopes, sticky notes, and other writing materials.
  - Printer and Printer Supplies
    - Printer, ink or toner, paper, printer maintenance kits, and cartridges.

Expense Categories

- **Office Expenses (continued)**
  - Computers
    - Computers, laptops, tablets
  - Monitors/keyboards/mouses/mousepads
  - Office Furniture
    - Desks, chairs, filing cabinets, bookshelves, or other furniture used exclusively for author work
  - Any office equipment/furniture that costs less than $2,500
  - Office Decor
    - Artwork, plants, or decorations enhancing the office ambiance.
  - Reference Materials
    - Books, magazines, online subscriptions, or reference materials relevant to writing, research, or professional development.
  - Shipping Supplies
    - Envelopes, packaging materials, postage stamps, and shipping labels for mailing manuscripts or promotional materials.
  - Office Cleaning Supplies
    - Cleaning agents, trash bags, wipes, or other supplies used to maintain a clean workspace.

Expense Categories

- **Office Expenses (continued)**
  - Organization and Storage
    - Folders, binders, dividers, filing systems, or storage boxes to keep manuscripts or documents organized.
  - Professional Memberships or Subscriptions
    - Membership fees for writing organizations, subscriptions to writing-related magazines, or online platforms.
  - Promotional Materials
    - Business cards, flyers, bookmarks, or promotional items used for marketing books or author brand.
      - *Though, this could also be under advertising (pick a place that makes sense to you and be consistent)*
  - Software Subscriptions
    - Writing-related subscriptions such as grammar checkers, cloud storage services, or project management tools.
  - Website Expenses
    - Domain registration, hosting fees, website design or maintenance costs for an author website or blog.
    - *Though, again, this could also be under advertising expense*

Expense Categories

- **Pension and Profit-Sharing Plans**
    - Your contributions to ***employee*** retirement plan
    - For employees' retirements, NOT YOURS
        - Your contributions to any retirement plans go on your 1040 in a different place, not on the schedule C
        - Same with your health insurance premiums - those don't go on your Schedule C
            - You can subtotal them and give them to your accountant to take elsewhere though!
            - Both your health insurance premiums and your dental premiums

- **Rent or Lease**
    - Rental expenses for business property
    - Office rent, equipment rents

- **Repairs and Maintenance**
    - Costs for repairing or maintaining business property
    - Laptop repairs
    - Office furniture repairs

Expense Categories

- **Supplies**
  - Costs of materials or supplies used in the business.
  - Or you could decide to make a 'Book Production Cost' category under the 'Miscellaneous Category' - your choice.

- **Taxes and Licenses**
  - Business-related taxes or licenses
  - Payroll taxes
  - Sales taxes
  - VAT

- **Travel**
  - Travel expenses for book signings, author events, or conferences
  - Registration fees for writing workshops or conferences
  - Travel expenses for research purposes

- **Meals**
  - Business-related meal expenses

Expense Categories

- **Utilities**
  - Costs for *business* utilities (electricity, phone, etc.).
  - UNLESS, they are home office utilities, then they go in that section. If you rent/own another place to work that is separate from your residence, this is where those expenses would go.
    - In my opinion, a shed out back, counts as a home office
  - **Hot tip: unless it's helpful to you, I recommend combining all types of utilities together in one 'Utilities' bucket.**
    - E.g. - Electricity, oil, sewer, water, internet, phone, etc. - can all go into one 'Utilities' bucket
      - No need to overcomplicate things

- **Wages**
  - Employee wages or salaries.
  - Again - not your *Draw* if you're filing a Schedule C - you take a 'draw' which is not an expense for your business. In fact, the IRS doesn't even want to know what you put in or took out of your business on your tax return. Instead, you're just taxed on the net income after expenses are taken out, regardless of whether you took that money out for your own purposes or not.

Expense Categories

You have the ability to create your own categories of expenses under "other expenses". Just try not to go too crazy with it. Try to fit it into an established category if you can.

- **Other Expenses**
  - **Miscellaneous expenses**
    - Reconciliation discrepancy
    - Contest or award entry fees
    - Research expenses
    - Promotional swag or giveaways
    - Bad debt - you paid someone who ghosted you
    - *These misc expenses can sometimes can be put into 'Office expense' depending on what they are*
  - **Professional Development**
    - Writing courses or workshops
    - Membership fees for writing associations or groups
    - Coaching or mentoring fees
  - Vendor/Book Fairs

Expense Categories

- **Other Expenses (continued)**
  - **Book Production Costs:** (*This could also be argued as Supplies or Cost of Goods Sold)*
    - Copyright registration fees
    - Proofreading and copyediting
    - Cover designer fees
    - Book formatting services
    - ISBN purchases
    - Printing and distribution costs
    - Audiobook production fees
    - Editors
    - Etc.

Tax tip reminder: anything over $2,500 that was purchased during the year (furniture, equipment, etc) should probably *not* be put in one of these expense buckets and instead should be capitalized as an asset and then depreciated on your tax return. This does not include coaching/courses. Those can be put in the expense buckets even though they may be over the $2,500. Make a note somewhere so you don't forget to include that purchase at tax time.

Expense Categories

Here's the high-level list, one more time

- Advertising
- Car and Truck Expenses
- Commissions and Fees
- Contract Labor
- Depreciation
- Employee Benefits Program
- Insurance
- Interest
- Legal and Professional Services
- Office Expenses
- Pension and Profit-Sharing Plans
- Rent or Lease
- Repairs and Maintenance
- Supplies
- Taxes and Licenses
- Travel
- Meals and Entertainment
- Utilities
- Wages
- Other Expenses:
    - Miscellaneous expenses
    - Book Production Costs
    - Other **(but try not to create a bunch of new 'other' categories if you can. Use your best guess and put in the buckets above if possible)**

Home Office Information

At month-end, calculate the total home office expenses for each category for that month and use it to populate the monthly summary pages.

At year-end, add up all of the monthly summaries and populate the yearly total pages.

Home Office Deduction

This page is just for information purposes

Form **8829**

Department of the Treasury
Internal Revenue Service

Expenses for Business Use of Your Home

File only with Schedule C (Form 1040). Use a separate Form 8829 for each home you used for business during the year.

Go to *www.irs.gov/Form8829* for instructions and the latest information.

OMB No. 1545-0074

2024

Attachment Sequence No. **176**

Name(s) of proprietor(s) | **Your social security number**

Part I — Part of Your Home Used for Business

1	Area used regularly and exclusively for business, regularly for daycare, or for storage of inventory or product samples (see instructions)	1	
2	Total area of home	2	
3	Divide line 1 by line 2. Enter the result as a percentage	3	%
	For daycare facilities not used exclusively for business, go to line 4. All others, go to line 7.		
4	Multiply days used for daycare during year by hours used per day — 4 ___ hr.		
5	If you started or stopped using your home for daycare during the year, see instructions; otherwise, enter 8,784 — 5 ___ hr.		
6	Divide line 4 by line 5. Enter the result as a decimal amount — 6 ___ .		
7	Business percentage. For daycare facilities not used exclusively for business, multiply line 6 by line 3 (enter the result as a percentage). All others, enter the amount from line 3	7	%

Part II — Figure Your Allowable Deduction

8	Enter the amount from Schedule C, line 29, **plus** any gain derived from the business use of your home, **minus** any loss from the trade or business not derived from the business use of your home. See instructions.				8	
	See instructions for columns (a) and (b) before completing lines 9–22.		**(a)** Direct expenses	**(b)** Indirect expenses		
9	Casualty losses (see instructions)	9				
10	Deductible mortgage interest (see instructions)	10				
11	Real estate taxes (see instructions)	11				
12	Add lines 9, 10, and 11	12				
13	Multiply line 12, column (b), by line 7		13			
14	Add line 12, column (a), and line 13				14	
15	Subtract line 14 from line 8. If zero or less, enter -0-				15	
16	Excess mortgage interest (see instructions)	16				
17	Excess real estate taxes (see instructions)	17				
18	Insurance	18				
19	Rent	19				
20	Repairs and maintenance	20				
21	Utilities	21				
22	Other expenses (see instructions)	22				
23	Add lines 16 through 22	23				
24	Multiply line 23, column (b), by line 7		24			
25	Carryover of prior year operating expenses (see instructions)		25			
26	Add line 23, column (a), line 24, and line 25				26	
27	Allowable operating expenses. Enter the **smaller** of line 15 or line 26				27	
28	Limit on excess casualty losses and depreciation. Subtract line 27 from line 15				28	
29	Excess casualty losses (see instructions)		29			
30	Depreciation of your home from line 42 below		30			
31	Carryover of prior year excess casualty losses and depreciation (see instructions)		31			
32	Add lines 29 through 31				32	
33	Allowable excess casualty losses and depreciation. Enter the **smaller** of line 28 or line 32				33	
34	Add lines 14, 27, and 33				34	
35	Casualty loss portion, if any, from lines 14 and 33. Carry amount to **Form 4684**. See instructions				35	
36	**Allowable expenses for business use of your home.** Subtract line 35 from line 34. Enter here and on Schedule C, line 30. If your home was used for more than one business, see instructions				36	

Part III — Depreciation of Your Home

37	Enter the **smaller** of your home's adjusted basis or its fair market value. See instructions	37	
38	Value of land included on line 37	38	
39	Basis of building. Subtract line 38 from line 37	39	
40	Business basis of building. Multiply line 39 by line 7	40	
41	Depreciation percentage (see instructions)	41	%
42	Depreciation allowable (see instructions). Multiply line 40 by line 41. Enter here and on line 30 above	42	

Part IV — Carryover of Unallowed Expenses to 2025

43	Operating expenses. Subtract line 27 from line 26. If less than zero, enter -0-	43	
44	Excess casualty losses and depreciation. Subtract line 33 from line 32. If less than zero, enter -0-	44	

For Paperwork Reduction Act Notice, see your tax return instructions. Cat. No. 13232M Form **8829** (2024)

Home Office Deduction

Ok, don't panic. Let's break it down

***Remember - this area has to be exclusively for business**

Total square footage of your office - ____________

Total square footage of your home - ____________

Sq ft of office / sq. ft of home = percent you can potentially deduct - ______%

- If you have a mortgage, you might receive a Form 1098 - great! Give that to your accountant. It may have your property taxes, mortgage interest, insurance premiums, etc
- Any big repairs/improvements to your home (over $2,500) tell your accountant.

- **Tax tip - give a copy of your Home Office Totals page to your accountant at tax time.**

- **Don't double count the expenses. If they're under H.O deductions, don't put them in the other expense categories as well**

Mileage Tracker

This area is just for mileage.

If you take mileage, **then you don't need to keep track of gas and other auto expenses like oil changes, tires, routine maintenance, or even big repairs like transmissions, etc.**

For simplicity, I'm going to assume you're just taking mileage, so **do not include those various actual auto expenses anywhere in this organizer**

Mileage Tracker

Odometer Mileage at Jan 1

____

Odometer Mileage at Dec 31

____

- Mileage rate per IRS = $0._____ per mile
- Here you can record any miles driven **for work**

Date	Miles Driven	Cumulative Total Miles

Mileage Tracker

Your accountant will be able to take your total mileage over the year (the difference in your beginning and ending odometer miles) and subtract your cumulative business mileage to get your personal miles driven. Not relevant for you - but it's relevant in terms of tax prep for your preparer

Date	Miles Driven	Cumulative Total Miles

Mileage Tracker

Date	Miles Driven	Cumulative Total Miles

Monthly Bookkeeping Trackers

January Income

JAN

For ease of use, I've populated some common sources of income for you
(I hope it helps cut down on your workload!)

Date	Income Source	Amount	Cumulative Total Income
	Amazon KDP		
	Amazon KDP		
	Amazon KDP		
	Amazon KDP		
	Amazon KDP		
	Amazon KDP		
	IngramSpark		
	Draft2Digital / SmashWords		
	Google Play		
	Kobo		
	Nook		

JAN

Date	Income Source	Amount	Total Income
	Apple		
	YouTube		
	Patreon		
	Kickstarter		
		Total Revenue for the month =	

January Expenses

JAN

Find the category that your expense belongs in and drop it in the applicable bucket.
Subtotal at the end of the month and populate the monthly summary

Date	Who did you pay?	Amount
Advertising Expenses: Costs for promoting the business, book promotions, Facebook ads, amazon ads, TikTok ads, website, book launches, etc		
	Total Expense =	

JAN

Date	Who did you pay?	Amount
Commissions: Agent commissions		
	Total Expense =	
Contract Labor: Payments to contractors or freelancers, royalty payments to co-authors or contributors		
	Total Expense =	

JAN

Date	Who did you pay?	Amount
Employee Benefit Programs: costs for employee health insurance		
	Total Expense =	
Insurance: costs of business insurance (<u>not</u> health, dental, home, car, etc)		
	Total Expense =	
Interest: Interest on business loans or credit cards (<u>not</u> your home mortgage interest or student loan interest)		
	Total Expense =	

JAN

Date	Who did you pay?	Amount
Legal and Professional Services: Legal or accounting fees for the business, CPA or tax preparation fees, Payroll processing fees, etc		
	Total Expense =	
Office Expenses: Supplies and expenses related to the business office, Stationery and Supplies, Pens, pencils, notebooks, notepads, paper, envelopes, sticky notes, and other writing materials, Printer and Printer Supplies, Computers, laptops, tablets, Monitors/keyboards/mouses/mousepads, Office Furniture, Any office equipment/furniture that costs less than $2,500, Office Décor, Reference Materials, Author software: Prowriting Aid, Grammarly, World Anvil, Trello, Microsoft, Software subscriptions, shipping, postage,		

JAN

Date	Who did you pay?	Amount
Office Expenses (continued): Supplies and expenses related to the business office, Stationery and Supplies, Pens, pencils, notebooks, notepads, paper, envelopes, sticky notes, and other writing materials, Printer and Printer Supplies, Computers, laptops, tablets, Monitors/keyboards/mouses/ mousepads, Office Furniture, Any office equipment/furniture that costs less than $2,500, Office Décor, Reference Materials, Author software: Prowriting Aid, Grammarly, World Anvil, Trello, Microsoft, Software subscriptions, etc		
	Total Expense =	

JAN

Date	Who did you pay?	Amount
Pension and Profit-Sharing Plans: your business's contributions to employee retirement plans		
	Total Expense =	
Rent: Costs to rent office space, equipment, etc		
	Total Expense =	
Repairs and Maintenance: Costs for repairing or maintaining business property, Laptop repairs, Office furniture repairs		
	Total Expense =	

JAN

Date	Who did you pay?	Amount
Taxes and Licenses: Business-related taxes or licenses, LLC registration, Payroll taxes, Sales taxes, VAT		
	Total Expense =	
Travel: Travel for book signings, author events, or conferences; Registration fees for writing workshops or conferences, Travel for research purposes		
	Total Expense =	
Meals: Business-related meal expenses		
	Total Expense =	

JAN

Date	Who did you pay?	Amount
Utilities: Costs for business utilities if you have an office you rent (electricity, phone, etc.) (not home office utilities)		
	Total Expense =	
Wages: Employee wages or salaries (not your Draw)		
	Total Expense =	
Miscellaneous: Professional development, author classes, etc. (you don't know where to put it, put it here)		
	Total Expense =	

JAN

Date	Who did you pay?	Amount
Book Production Costs: Copyright registration fees, Proofreading and copyediting, Cover designer fees, Book formatting services, ISBN purchases, Printing and distribution costs, Audiobook production fees, Editors, Etc.		
	Total Expense =	

JAN

Here are some extra pages just in case you need more space!

Date	Who did you pay?	Amount	Category

JAN

Here are some extra pages just in case you need more space!

Date	Who did you pay?	Amount	Category

January Home Office

This is the are where you keep track of your home office deductions. Do not put them with the regular expenses.
At month-end, calculate the subtotals and use it to populate the monthly summary page.
At year-end, add up all of the monthly summaries and populate the yearly total pages.

JAN

Date	Who did you pay?	Amount
Electric		
	Total Expense =	
Water/Sewer		
	Total Expense =	
Heating/Oil/Cooling		
	Total Expense =	
Internet/Phone		
	Total Expense =	
Trash/Recycling		
	Total Expense =	

JAN

Date	Who did you pay?	Amount
Home security		
	Total Expense =	
Plowing		
	Total Expense =	
Lawn Maintenance		
	Total Expense =	
Repairs (to home and to office)		
	Total Expense =	
Other		
	Total Expense =	

January Totals

January Home Office Totals

	Amount
Electric	
Water/Sewer	
Heating/Oil/Cooling	
Internet/Phone	
Trash/Recycling	
Home security	
Plowing	
Lawn Maintenance	
Repairs (to home and to office)	
Other	

Add up all of the monthly summary pages to populate the yearly summary sheets

January Income Statement

(Profit & Loss)

	Amount
Total Revenues	
Expenses:	
Advertising	
Car/truck expenses	
Commissions and fees	
Contract labor	
Depreciation	
Employee benefit programs	
Insurance	
Interest	
Legal and Professional	
Office Expense	
Pension/profit-sharing	
Rent/Lease	
Repairs & Maintenance	
Supplies	
Taxes & Licenses	
Travel (not mileage or gas)	
Meals	
Entertainment	
Utilities	
Wages	
Miscellaneous	
Book Production Costs	
Total Expenses	
Net Income (revenue - expenses)	

February Income

FEB

For ease of use, I've populated some common sources of income for you
(I hope it helps cut down on your workload!)

Date	Income Source	Amount	Cumulative Total Income
	Amazon KDP		
	Amazon KDP		
	Amazon KDP		
	Amazon KDP		
	Amazon KDP		
	Amazon KDP		
	IngramSpark		
	Draft2Digital / SmashWords		
	Google Play		
	Kobo		
	Nook		

FEB

Date	Income Source	Amount	Total Income
	Apple		
	YouTube		
	Patreon		
	Kickstarter		
		Total Revenue for the month =	

February Expenses

FEB

Find the category that your expense belongs in and drop it in the applicable bucket.
Subtotal at the end of the month and populate the monthly summary

Date	Who did you pay?	Amount
Advertising Expenses: Costs for promoting the business, book promotions, Facebook ads, amazon ads, TikTok ads, website, book launches, etc		
	Total Expense =	

FEB

Date	Who did you pay?	Amount
Commissions: Agent commissions		
	Total Expense =	
Contract Labor: Payments to contractors or freelancers, royalty payments to co-authors or contributors		
	Total Expense =	

FEB

Date	Who did you pay?	Amount
Employee Benefit Programs: costs for employee health insurance		
	Total Expense =	
Insurance: costs of business insurance (not health, dental, home, car, etc)		
	Total Expense =	
Interest: Interest on business loans or credit cards (not your home mortgage interest or student loan interest)		
	Total Expense =	

FEB

Date	Who did you pay?	Amount
Legal and Professional Services: Legal or accounting fees for the business, CPA or tax preparation fees, Payroll processing fees, etc		
	Total Expense =	
Office Expenses: Supplies and expenses related to the business office, Stationery and Supplies, Pens, pencils, notebooks, notepads, paper, envelopes, sticky notes, and other writing materials, Printer and Printer Supplies, Computers, laptops, tablets, Monitors/keyboards/mouses/mousepads, Office Furniture, Any office equipment/furniture that costs less than $2,500, Office Décor, Reference Materials, Author software: Prowriting Aid, Grammarly, World Anvil, Trello, Microsoft, Software subscriptions, shipping, postage,		

FEB

Date	Who did you pay?	Amount
Office Expenses (continued): Supplies and expenses related to the business office, Stationery and Supplies, Pens, pencils, notebooks, notepads, paper, envelopes, sticky notes, and other writing materials, Printer and Printer Supplies, Computers, laptops, tablets, Monitors/keyboards/mouses/ mousepads, Office Furniture, Any office equipment/furniture that costs less than $2,500, Office Décor, Reference Materials, Author software: Prowriting Aid, Grammarly, World Anvil, Trello, Microsoft, Software subscriptions, etc		
	Total Expense =	

FEB

Date	Who did you pay?	Amount
Pension and Profit-Sharing Plans: your business's contributions to employee retirement plans		
	Total Expense =	
Rent: Costs to rent office space, equipment, etc		
	Total Expense =	
Repairs and Maintenance: Costs for repairing or maintaining business property, Laptop repairs, Office furniture repairs		
	Total Expense =	

FEB

Date	Who did you pay?	Amount
Taxes and Licenses: Business-related taxes or licenses, LLC registration, Payroll taxes, Sales taxes, VAT		
	Total Expense =	
Travel: Travel for book signings, author events, or conferences; Registration fees for writing workshops or conferences, Travel for research purposes		
	Total Expense =	
Meals: Business-related meal expenses		
	Total Expense =	

FEB

Date	Who did you pay?	Amount
Utilities: Costs for business utilities if you have an office you rent (electricity, phone, etc.) (not home office utilities)		
	Total Expense =	
Wages: Employee wages or salaries (not your Draw)		
	Total Expense =	
Miscellaneous: Professional development, author classes, etc. (you don't know where to put it, put it here)		
	Total Expense =	

FEB

Date	Who did you pay?	Amount
Book Production Costs: Copyright registration fees, Proofreading and copyediting, Cover designer fees, Book formatting services, ISBN purchases, Printing and distribution costs, Audiobook production fees, Editors, Etc.		
	Total Expense =	

FEB

Here are some extra pages just in case you need more space!

Date	Who did you pay?	Amount	Category

FEB

Here are some extra pages just in case you need more space!

Date	Who did you pay?	Amount	Category

February Home Office

FEB

Date	Who did you pay?	Amount
Electric		
	Total Expense =	
Water/Sewer		
	Total Expense =	
Heating/Oil/Cooling		
	Total Expense =	
Internet/Phone		
	Total Expense =	
Trash/Recycling		
	Total Expense =	

FEB

Date	Who did you pay?	Amount
Home security		
	Total Expense =	
Plowing		
	Total Expense =	
Lawn Maintenance		
	Total Expense =	
Repairs (to home and to office)		
	Total Expense =	
Other		
	Total Expense =	

February Totals

February Home Office Totals

	Amount
Electric	
Water/Sewer	
Heating/Oil/Cooling	
Internet/Phone	
Trash/Recycling	
Home security	
Plowing	
Lawn Maintenance	
Repairs (to home and to office)	
Other	

February Income Statement

(Monthly Profit & Loss)

	Amount
Total Revenues	
Expenses:	
Advertising	
Car/truck expenses	
Commissions and fees	
Contract labor	
Depreciation	
Employee benefit programs	
Insurance	
Interest	
Legal and Professional	
Office Expense	
Pension/profit-sharing	
Rent/Lease	
Repairs & Maintenance	
Supplies	
Taxes & Licenses	
Travel (not mileage or gas)	
Meals	
Entertainment	
Utilities	
Wages	
Miscellaneous	
Book Production Costs	
Total Expenses	
Net Income (revenue - expenses)	

March Income

MAR

For ease of use, I've populated some common sources of income for you (I hope it helps cut down on your workload!)

Date	Income Source	Amount	Cumulative Total Income
	Amazon KDP		
	Amazon KDP		
	Amazon KDP		
	Amazon KDP		
	Amazon KDP		
	Amazon KDP		
	IngramSpark		
	Draft2Digital / SmashWords		
	Google Play		
	Kobo		
	Nook		

MAR

Date	Income Source	Amount	Total Income
	Apple		
	YouTube		
	Patreon		
	Kickstarter		
		Total Revenue for the month =	

March Expenses

MAR

Find the category that your expense belongs in and drop it in the applicable bucket.
Subtotal at the end of the month and populate the monthly summary

Date	Who did you pay?	Amount
Advertising Expenses: Costs for promoting the business, book promotions, Facebook ads, amazon ads, TikTok ads, website, book launches, etc		
	Total Expense =	

MAR

Date	Who did you pay?	Amount
Commissions: Agent commissions		
	Total Expense =	
Contract Labor: Payments to contractors or freelancers, royalty payments to co-authors or contributors		
	Total Expense =	

MAR

Date	Who did you pay?	Amount
Employee Benefit Programs: costs for employee health insurance		
	Total Expense =	
Insurance: costs of business insurance (<u>not</u> health, dental, home, car, etc)		
	Total Expense =	
Interest: Interest on business loans or credit cards (<u>not</u> your home mortgage interest or student loan interest)		
	Total Expense =	

MAR

Date	Who did you pay?	Amount
Legal and Professional Services: Legal or accounting fees for the business, CPA or tax preparation fees, Payroll processing fees, etc		
	Total Expense =	
Office Expenses: Supplies and expenses related to the business office, Stationery and Supplies, Pens, pencils, notebooks, notepads, paper, envelopes, sticky notes, and other writing materials, Printer and Printer Supplies, Computers, laptops, tablets, Monitors/keyboards/mouses/mousepads, Office Furniture, Any office equipment/furniture that costs less than $2,500, Office Décor, Reference Materials, Author software: Prowriting Aid, Grammarly, World Anvil, Trello, Microsoft, Software subscriptions, shipping, postage,		

MAR

Date	Who did you pay?	Amount
Office Expenses (continued): Supplies and expenses related to the business office, Stationery and Supplies, Pens, pencils, notebooks, notepads, paper, envelopes, sticky notes, and other writing materials, Printer and Printer Supplies, Computers, laptops, tablets, Monitors/keyboards/mouses/ mousepads, Office Furniture, Any office equipment/furniture that costs less than $2,500, Office Décor, Reference Materials, Author software: Prowriting Aid, Grammarly, World Anvil, Trello, Microsoft, Software subscriptions, etc		
	Total Expense =	

MAR

Date	Who did you pay?	Amount
Pension and Profit-Sharing Plans: your business's contributions to employee retirement plans		
	Total Expense =	
Rent: Costs to rent office space, equipment, etc		
	Total Expense =	
Repairs and Maintenance: Costs for repairing or maintaining business property, Laptop repairs, Office furniture repairs		
	Total Expense =	

MAR

Date	Who did you pay?	Amount
Taxes and Licenses: Business-related taxes or licenses, LLC registration, Payroll taxes, Sales taxes, VAT		
	Total Expense =	
Travel: Travel for book signings, author events, or conferences; Registration fees for writing workshops or conferences, Travel for research purposes		
	Total Expense =	
Meals: Business-related meal expenses		
	Total Expense =	

MAR

Date	Who did you pay?	Amount
Utilities: Costs for business utilities if you have an office you rent (electricity, phone, etc.) (not home office utilities)		
	Total Expense =	
Wages: Employee wages or salaries (not your Draw)		
	Total Expense =	
Miscellaneous: Professional development, author classes, etc. (you don't know where to put it, put it here)		
	Total Expense =	

MAR

Date	Who did you pay?	Amount
Book Production Costs: Copyright registration fees, Proofreading and copyediting, Cover designer fees, Book formatting services, ISBN purchases, Printing and distribution costs, Audiobook production fees, Editors, Etc.		
	Total Expense =	

MAR

Here are some extra pages just in case you need more space!

Date	Who did you pay?	Amount	Category

MAR

Here are some extra pages just in case you need more space!

Date	Who did you pay?	Amount	Category

March Home Office

MAR

Date	Who did you pay?	Amount
Electric		
	Total Expense =	
Water/Sewer		
	Total Expense =	
Heating/Oil/Cooling		
	Total Expense =	
Internet/Phone		
	Total Expense =	
Trash/Recycling		
	Total Expense =	

MAR

Date	Who did you pay?	Amount
Home security		
	Total Expense =	
Plowing		
	Total Expense =	
Lawn Maintenance		
	Total Expense =	
Repairs (to home and to office)		
	Total Expense =	
Other		
	Total Expense =	

March Totals

March Home Office Totals

	Amount
Electric	
Water/Sewer	
Heating/Oil/Cooling	
Internet/Phone	
Trash/Recycling	
Home security	
Plowing	
Lawn Maintenance	
Repairs (to home and to office)	
Other	

Add up all of the monthly summary pages to populate the yearly summary sheets

March Income Statement

(Profit & Loss)

	Amount
Total Revenues	
Expenses:	
Advertising	
Car/truck expenses	
Commissions and fees	
Contract labor	
Depreciation	
Employee benefit programs	
Insurance	
Interest	
Legal and Professional	
Office Expense	
Pension/profit-sharing	
Rent/Lease	
Repairs & Maintenance	
Supplies	
Taxes & Licenses	
Travel (not mileage or gas)	
Meals	
Entertainment	
Utilities	
Wages	
Miscellaneous	
Book Production Costs	
Total Expenses	
Net Income (revenue - expenses)	

April Income

APR

For ease of use, I've populated some common sources of income for you (I hope it helps cut down on your workload!)

Date	Income Source	Amount	Cumulative Total Income
	Amazon KDP		
	Amazon KDP		
	Amazon KDP		
	Amazon KDP		
	Amazon KDP		
	Amazon KDP		
	IngramSpark		
	Draft2Digital / SmashWords		
	Google Play		
	Kobo		
	Nook		

APR

Date	Income Source	Amount	Total Income
	Apple		
	YouTube		
	Patreon		
	Kickstarter		
		Total Revenue for the month =	

April Expenses

APR

Find the category that your expense belongs in and drop it in the applicable bucket.
Subtotal at the end of the month and populate the monthly summary

Date	Who did you pay?	Amount
Advertising Expenses: Costs for promoting the business, book promotions, Facebook ads, amazon ads, TikTok ads, website, book launches, etc		
	Total Expense =	

APR

Date	Who did you pay?	Amount
Commissions: Agent commissions		
	Total Expense =	
Contract Labor: Payments to contractors or freelancers, royalty payments to co-authors or contributors		
	Total Expense =	

APR

Date	Who did you pay?	Amount
Employee Benefit Programs: costs for employee health insurance		
	Total Expense =	
Insurance: costs of business insurance (<u>not</u> health, dental, home, car, etc)		
	Total Expense =	
Interest: Interest on business loans or credit cards (<u>not</u> your home mortgage interest or student loan interest)		
	Total Expense =	

APR

Date	Who did you pay?	Amount
Legal and Professional Services: Legal or accounting fees for the business, CPA or tax preparation fees, Payroll processing fees, etc		
	Total Expense =	
Office Expenses: Supplies and expenses related to the business office, Stationery and Supplies, Pens, pencils, notebooks, notepads, paper, envelopes, sticky notes, and other writing materials, Printer and Printer Supplies, Computers, laptops, tablets, Monitors/keyboards/mouses/mousepads, Office Furniture, Any office equipment/furniture that costs less than $2,500, Office Décor, Reference Materials, Author software: Prowriting Aid, Grammarly, World Anvil, Trello, Microsoft, Software subscriptions, shipping, postage.		

APR

Date	Who did you pay?	Amount
Office Expenses (continued): Supplies and expenses related to the business office, Stationery and Supplies, Pens, pencils, notebooks, notepads, paper, envelopes, sticky notes, and other writing materials, Printer and Printer Supplies, Computers, laptops, tablets, Monitors/keyboards/mouses/ mousepads, Office Furniture, Any office equipment/furniture that costs less than $2,500, Office Décor, Reference Materials, Author software: Prowriting Aid, Grammarly, World Anvil, Trello, Microsoft, Software subscriptions, etc		
	Total Expense =	

APR

Date	Who did you pay?	Amount
Pension and Profit-Sharing Plans: your business's contributions to employee retirement plans		
	Total Expense =	
Rent: Costs to rent office space, equipment, etc		
	Total Expense =	
Repairs and Maintenance: Costs for repairing or maintaining business property, Laptop repairs, Office furniture repairs		
	Total Expense =	

APR

Date	Who did you pay?	Amount
Taxes and Licenses: Business-related taxes or licenses, LLC registration, Payroll taxes, Sales taxes, VAT		
	Total Expense =	
Travel: Travel for book signings, author events, or conferences; Registration fees for writing workshops or conferences, Travel for research purposes		
	Total Expense =	
Meals: Business-related meal expenses		
	Total Expense =	

APR

Date	Who did you pay?	Amount
Utilities: Costs for business utilities if you have an office you rent (electricity, phone, etc.) (not home office utilities)		
	Total Expense =	
Wages: Employee wages or salaries (not your Draw)		
	Total Expense =	
Miscellaneous: Professional development, author classes, etc. (you don't know where to put it, put it here)		
	Total Expense =	

APR

Date	Who did you pay?	Amount
Book Production Costs: Copyright registration fees, Proofreading and copyediting, Cover designer fees, Book formatting services, ISBN purchases, Printing and distribution costs, Audiobook production fees, Editors, Etc.		
	Total Expense =	

APR

Here are some extra pages just in case you need more space!

Date	Who did you pay?	Amount	Category

APR

Here are some extra pages just in case you need more space!

Date	Who did you pay?	Amount	Category

April
Home Office

APR

Date	Who did you pay?	Amount
Electric		
	Total Expense =	
Water/Sewer		
	Total Expense =	
Heating/Oil/Cooling		
	Total Expense =	
Internet/Phone		
	Total Expense =	
Trash/Recycling		
	Total Expense =	

APR

Date	Who did you pay?	Amount
Home security		
	Total Expense =	
Plowing		
	Total Expense =	
Lawn Maintenance		
	Total Expense =	
Repairs (to home and to office)		
	Total Expense =	
Other		
	Total Expense =	

April Totals

April Home Office Totals

	Amount
Electric	
Water/Sewer	
Heating/Oil/Cooling	
Internet/Phone	
Trash/Recycling	
Home security	
Plowing	
Lawn Maintenance	
Repairs (to home and to office)	
Other	

Add up all of the monthly summary pages to populate the yearly summary sheets

April Income Statement

(Profit & Loss)

	Amount
Total Revenues	
Expenses:	
Advertising	
Car/truck expenses	
Commissions and fees	
Contract labor	
Depreciation	
Employee benefit programs	
Insurance	
Interest	
Legal and Professional	
Office Expense	
Pension/profit-sharing	
Rent/Lease	
Repairs & Maintenance	
Supplies	
Taxes & Licenses	
Travel (not mileage or gas)	
Meals	
Entertainment	
Utilities	
Wages	
Miscellaneous	
Book Production Costs	
Total Expenses	
Net Income (revenue - expenses)	

May Income

MAY

For ease of use, I've populated some common sources of income for you (I hope it helps cut down on your workload!)

Date	Income Source	Amount	Cumulative Total Income
	Amazon KDP		
	Amazon KDP		
	Amazon KDP		
	Amazon KDP		
	Amazon KDP		
	Amazon KDP		
	IngramSpark		
	Draft2Digital / SmashWords		
	Google Play		
	Kobo		
	Nook		

MAY

Date	Income Source	Amount	Total Income
	Apple		
	YouTube		
	Patreon		
	Kickstarter		
		Total Revenue for the month =	

May Expenses

MAY

Find the category that your expense belongs in and drop it in the applicable bucket. Subtotal at the end of the month and populate the monthly summary

Date	Who did you pay?	Amount
Advertising Expenses: Costs for promoting the business, book promotions, Facebook ads, amazon ads, TikTok ads, website, book launches, etc		
	Total Expense =	

MAY

Date	Who did you pay?	Amount
Commissions: Agent commissions		
	Total Expense =	
Contract Labor: Payments to contractors or freelancers, royalty payments to co-authors or contributors		
	Total Expense =	

MAY

Date	Who did you pay?	Amount
Employee Benefit Programs: costs for employee health insurance		
	Total Expense =	
Insurance: costs of business insurance (not health, dental, home, car, etc)		
	Total Expense =	
Interest: Interest on business loans or credit cards (not your home mortgage interest or student loan interest)		
	Total Expense =	

MAY

Date	Who did you pay?	Amount
Legal and Professional Services: Legal or accounting fees for the business, CPA or tax preparation fees, Payroll processing fees, etc		
	Total Expense =	
Office Expenses: Supplies and expenses related to the business office, Stationery and Supplies, Pens, pencils, notebooks, notepads, paper, envelopes, sticky notes, and other writing materials, Printer and Printer Supplies, Computers, laptops, tablets, Monitors/keyboards/mouses/mousepads, Office Furniture, Any office equipment/furniture that costs less than $2,500, Office Décor, Reference Materials, Author software: Prowriting Aid, Grammarly, World Anvil, Trello, Microsoft, Software subscriptions, shipping, postage,		

MAY

Date	Who did you pay?	Amount
Office Expenses (continued): Supplies and expenses related to the business office, Stationery and Supplies, Pens, pencils, notebooks, notepads, paper, envelopes, sticky notes, and other writing materials, Printer and Printer Supplies, Computers, laptops, tablets, Monitors/keyboards/mouses/mousepads, Office Furniture, Any office equipment/furniture that costs less than $2,500, Office Décor, Reference Materials, Author software: Prowriting Aid, Grammarly, World Anvil, Trello, Microsoft, Software subscriptions, etc		
	Total Expense =	

MAY

Date	Who did you pay?	Amount
Pension and Profit-Sharing Plans: your business's contributions to employee retirement plans		
	Total Expense =	
Rent: Costs to rent office space, equipment, etc		
	Total Expense =	
Repairs and Maintenance: Costs for repairing or maintaining business property, Laptop repairs, Office furniture repairs		
	Total Expense =	

MAY

Date	Who did you pay?	Amount
Taxes and Licenses: Business-related taxes or licenses, LLC registration, Payroll taxes, Sales taxes, VAT		
	Total Expense =	
Travel: Travel for book signings, author events, or conferences; Registration fees for writing workshops or conferences, Travel for research purposes		
	Total Expense =	
Meals: Business-related meal expenses		
	Total Expense =	

MAY

Date	Who did you pay?	Amount
Utilities: Costs for business utilities if you have an office you rent (electricity, phone, etc.) (not home office utilities)		
	Total Expense =	
Wages: Employee wages or salaries (not your Draw)		
	Total Expense =	
Miscellaneous: Professional development, author classes, etc. (you don't know where to put it, put it here)		
	Total Expense =	

MAY

Date	Who did you pay?	Amount
Book Production Costs: Copyright registration fees, Proofreading and copyediting, Cover designer fees, Book formatting services, ISBN purchases, Printing and distribution costs, Audiobook production fees, Editors, Etc.		
	Total Expense =	

MAY

Here are some extra pages just in case you need more space!

Date	Who did you pay?	Amount	Category

MAY

Here are some extra pages just in case you need more space!

Date	Who did you pay?	Amount	Category

May
Home Office

MAY

Date	Who did you pay?	Amount
Electric		
	Total Expense =	
Water/Sewer		
	Total Expense =	
Heating/Oil/Cooling		
	Total Expense =	
Internet/Phone		
	Total Expense =	
Trash/Recycling		
	Total Expense =	

MAY

Date	Who did you pay?	Amount
Home security		
	Total Expense =	
Plowing		
	Total Expense =	
Lawn Maintenance		
	Total Expense =	
Repairs (to home and to office)		
	Total Expense =	
Other		
	Total Expense =	

May Totals

May Home Office Totals

	Amount
Electric	
Water/Sewer	
Heating/Oil/Cooling	
Internet/Phone	
Trash/Recycling	
Home security	
Plowing	
Lawn Maintenance	
Repairs (to home and to office)	
Other	

Add up all of the monthly summary pages to populate the yearly summary sheets

May Income Statement

(Profit & Loss)

	Amount
Total Revenues	
Expenses:	
Advertising	
Car/truck expenses	
Commissions and fees	
Contract labor	
Depreciation	
Employee benefit programs	
Insurance	
Interest	
Legal and Professional	
Office Expense	
Pension/profit-sharing	
Rent/Lease	
Repairs & Maintenance	
Supplies	
Taxes & Licenses	
Travel (not mileage or gas)	
Meals	
Entertainment	
Utilities	
Wages	
Miscellaneous	
Book Production Costs	
Total Expenses	
Net Income (revenue - expenses)	

June Income

JUN

For ease of use, I've populated some common sources of income for you (I hope it helps cut down on your workload!)

Date	Income Source	Amount	Cumulative Total Income
	Amazon KDP		
	Amazon KDP		
	Amazon KDP		
	Amazon KDP		
	Amazon KDP		
	Amazon KDP		
	IngramSpark		
	Draft2Digital / SmashWords		
	Google Play		
	Kobo		
	Nook		

JUN

Date	Income Source	Amount	Total Income
	Apple		
	YouTube		
	Patreon		
	Kickstarter		
		Total Revenue for the month =	

June Expenses

JUN

Find the category that your expense belongs in and drop it in the applicable bucket. Subtotal at the end of the month and populate the monthly summary

Date	Who did you pay?	Amount
Advertising Expenses: Costs for promoting the business, book promotions, Facebook ads, amazon ads, TikTok ads, website, book launches, etc		
	Total Expense =	

JUN

Date	Who did you pay?	Amount
Commissions: Agent commissions		
	Total Expense =	
Contract Labor: Payments to contractors or freelancers, royalty payments to co-authors or contributors		
	Total Expense =	

JUN

Date	Who did you pay?	Amount
Employee Benefit Programs: costs for employee health insurance		
	Total Expense =	
Insurance: costs of business insurance (<u>not</u> health, dental, home, car, etc)		
	Total Expense =	
Interest: Interest on business loans or credit cards (<u>not</u> your home mortgage interest or student loan interest)		
	Total Expense =	

JUN

Date	Who did you pay?	Amount
Legal and Professional Services: Legal or accounting fees for the business, CPA or tax preparation fees, Payroll processing fees, etc		
	Total Expense =	
Office Expenses: Supplies and expenses related to the business office, Stationery and Supplies, Pens, pencils, notebooks, notepads, paper, envelopes, sticky notes, and other writing materials, Printer and Printer Supplies, Computers, laptops, tablets, Monitors/keyboards/mouses/mousepads, Office Furniture, Any office equipment/furniture that costs less than $2,500, Office Décor, Reference Materials, Author software: Prowriting Aid, Grammarly, World Anvil, Trello, Microsoft, Software subscriptions, shipping, postage.		

JUN

Date	Who did you pay?	Amount
Office Expenses (continued): Supplies and expenses related to the business office, Stationery and Supplies, Pens, pencils, notebooks, notepads, paper, envelopes, sticky notes, and other writing materials, Printer and Printer Supplies, Computers, laptops, tablets, Monitors/keyboards/mouses/ mousepads, Office Furniture, Any office equipment/furniture that costs less than $2,500, Office Décor, Reference Materials, Author software: Prowriting Aid, Grammarly, World Anvil, Trello, Microsoft, Software subscriptions, etc		
	Total Expense =	

JUN

Date	Who did you pay?	Amount
Pension and Profit-Sharing Plans: your business's contributions to employee retirement plans		
	Total Expense =	
Rent: Costs to rent office space, equipment, etc		
	Total Expense =	
Repairs and Maintenance: Costs for repairing or maintaining business property, Laptop repairs, Office furniture repairs		
	Total Expense =	

JUN

Date	Who did you pay?	Amount
Taxes and Licenses: Business-related taxes or licenses, LLC registration, Payroll taxes, Sales taxes, VAT		
	Total Expense =	
Travel: Travel for book signings, author events, or conferences; Registration fees for writing workshops or conferences, Travel for research purposes		
	Total Expense =	
Meals: Business-related meal expenses		
	Total Expense =	

JUN

Date	Who did you pay?	Amount
Utilities: Costs for business utilities if you have an office you rent (electricity, phone, etc.) (not home office utilities)		
	Total Expense =	
Wages: Employee wages or salaries (not your Draw)		
	Total Expense =	
Miscellaneous: Professional development, author classes, etc. (you don't know where to put it, put it here)		
	Total Expense =	

JUN

Date	Who did you pay?	Amount
Book Production Costs: Copyright registration fees, Proofreading and copyediting, Cover designer fees, Book formatting services, ISBN purchases, Printing and distribution costs, Audiobook production fees, Editors, Etc.		
	Total Expense =	

JUN

Here are some extra pages just in case you need more space!

Date	Who did you pay?	Amount	Category

JUN

Here are some extra pages just in case you need more space!

Date	Who did you pay?	Amount	Category

June
Home Office

JUN

Date	Who did you pay?	Amount
Electric		
	Total Expense =	
Water/Sewer		
	Total Expense =	
Heating/Oil/Cooling		
	Total Expense =	
Internet/Phone		
	Total Expense =	
Trash/Recycling		
	Total Expense =	

JUN

Date	Who did you pay?	Amount
Home security		
	Total Expense =	
Plowing		
	Total Expense =	
Lawn Maintenance		
	Total Expense =	
Repairs (to home and to office)		
	Total Expense =	
Other		
	Total Expense =	

June Totals

June Home Office Totals

	Amount
Electric	
Water/Sewer	
Heating/Oil/Cooling	
Internet/Phone	
Trash/Recycling	
Home security	
Plowing	
Lawn Maintenance	
Repairs (to home and to office)	
Other	

Add up all of the monthly summary pages to populate the yearly summary sheets

June Income Statement

(Profit & Loss)

	Amount
Total Revenues	
Expenses:	
Advertising	
Car/truck expenses	
Commissions and fees	
Contract labor	
Depreciation	
Employee benefit programs	
Insurance	
Interest	
Legal and Professional	
Office Expense	
Pension/profit-sharing	
Rent/Lease	
Repairs & Maintenance	
Supplies	
Taxes & Licenses	
Travel (not mileage or gas)	
Meals	
Entertainment	
Utilities	
Wages	
Miscellaneous	
Book Production Costs	
Total Expenses	
Net Income (revenue - expenses)	

July
Income

JUL

For ease of use, I've populated some common sources of income for you (I hope it helps cut down on your workload!)

Date	Income Source	Amount	Cumulative Total Income
	Amazon KDP		
	Amazon KDP		
	Amazon KDP		
	Amazon KDP		
	Amazon KDP		
	Amazon KDP		
	IngramSpark		
	Draft2Digital / SmashWords		
	Google Play		
	Kobo		
	Nook		

JUL

Date	Income Source	Amount	Total Income
	Apple		
	YouTube		
	Patreon		
	Kickstarter		
		Total Revenue for the month =	

July Expenses

JUL

Find the category that your expense belongs in and drop it in the applicable bucket.
Subtotal at the end of the month and populate the monthly summary

Date	Who did you pay?	Amount
Advertising Expenses: Costs for promoting the business, book promotions, Facebook ads, amazon ads, TikTok ads, website, book launches, etc		
	Total Expense =	

JUL

Date	Who did you pay?	Amount
Commissions: Agent commissions		
	Total Expense =	
Contract Labor: Payments to contractors or freelancers, royalty payments to co-authors or contributors		
	Total Expense =	

JUL

Date	Who did you pay?	Amount
Employee Benefit Programs: costs for employee health insurance		
	Total Expense =	
Insurance: costs of business insurance (not health, dental, home, car, etc)		
	Total Expense =	
Interest: Interest on business loans or credit cards (not your home mortgage interest or student loan interest)		
	Total Expense =	

JUL

Date	Who did you pay?	Amount
Legal and Professional Services: Legal or accounting fees for the business, CPA or tax preparation fees, Payroll processing fees, etc		
	Total Expense =	
Office Expenses: Supplies and expenses related to the business office, Stationery and Supplies, Pens, pencils, notebooks, notepads, paper, envelopes, sticky notes, and other writing materials, Printer and Printer Supplies, Computers, laptops, tablets, Monitors/keyboards/mouses/mousepads, Office Furniture, Any office equipment/furniture that costs less than $2,500, Office Décor, Reference Materials, Author software: Prowriting Aid, Grammarly, World Anvil, Trello, Microsoft, Software subscriptions, shipping, postage.		

JUL

Date	Who did you pay?	Amount
Office Expenses (continued): Supplies and expenses related to the business office, Stationery and Supplies, Pens, pencils, notebooks, notepads, paper, envelopes, sticky notes, and other writing materials, Printer and Printer Supplies, Computers, laptops, tablets, Monitors/keyboards/mouses/mousepads, Office Furniture, Any office equipment/furniture that costs less than $2,500, Office Décor, Reference Materials, Author software: Prowriting Aid, Grammarly, World Anvil, Trello, Microsoft, Software subscriptions, etc		
	Total Expense =	

JUL

Date	Who did you pay?	Amount
Pension and Profit-Sharing Plans: your business's contributions to employee retirement plans		
	Total Expense =	
Rent: Costs to rent office space, equipment, etc		
	Total Expense =	
Repairs and Maintenance: Costs for repairing or maintaining business property, Laptop repairs, Office furniture repairs		
	Total Expense =	

JUL

Date	Who did you pay?	Amount
Taxes and Licenses: Business-related taxes or licenses, LLC registration, Payroll taxes, Sales taxes, VAT		
	Total Expense =	
Travel: Travel for book signings, author events, or conferences; Registration fees for writing workshops or conferences, Travel for research purposes		
	Total Expense =	
Meals: Business-related meal expenses		
	Total Expense =	

JUL

Date	Who did you pay?	Amount
Utilities: Costs for business utilities if you have an office you rent (electricity, phone, etc.) (not home office utilities)		
	Total Expense =	
Wages: Employee wages or salaries (not your Draw)		
	Total Expense =	
Miscellaneous: Professional development, author classes, etc. (you don't know where to put it, put it here)		
	Total Expense =	

JUL

Date	Who did you pay?	Amount
Book Production Costs: Copyright registration fees, Proofreading and copyediting, Cover designer fees, Book formatting services, ISBN purchases, Printing and distribution costs, Audiobook production fees, Editors, Etc.		
	Total Expense =	

JUL

Here are some extra pages just in case you need more space!

Date	Who did you pay?	Amount	Category

JUL

Here are some extra pages just in case you need more space!

Date	Who did you pay?	Amount	Category

July
Home Office

JUL

Date	Who did you pay?	Amount
Electric		
	Total Expense =	
Water/Sewer		
	Total Expense =	
Heating/Oil/Cooling		
	Total Expense =	
Internet/Phone		
	Total Expense =	
Trash/Recycling		
	Total Expense =	

JUL

Date	Who did you pay?	Amount
Home security		
	Total Expense =	
Plowing		
	Total Expense =	
Lawn Maintenance		
	Total Expense =	
Repairs (to home and to office)		
	Total Expense =	
Other		
	Total Expense =	

July Totals

July Home Office Totals

	Amount
Electric	
Water/Sewer	
Heating/Oil/Cooling	
Internet/Phone	
Trash/Recycling	
Home security	
Plowing	
Lawn Maintenance	
Repairs (to home and to office)	
Other	

Add up all of the monthly summary pages to populate the yearly summary sheets

July Income Statement

(Profit & Loss)

	Amount
Total Revenues	
Expenses:	
Advertising	
Car/truck expenses	
Commissions and fees	
Contract labor	
Depreciation	
Employee benefit programs	
Insurance	
Interest	
Legal and Professional	
Office Expense	
Pension/profit-sharing	
Rent/Lease	
Repairs & Maintenance	
Supplies	
Taxes & Licenses	
Travel (not mileage or gas)	
Meals	
Entertainment	
Utilities	
Wages	
Miscellaneous	
Book Production Costs	
Total Expenses	
Net Income (revenue - expenses)	

August Income

AUG

For ease of use, I've populated some common sources of income for you (I hope it helps cut down on your workload!)

Date	Income Source	Amount	Cumulative Total Income
	Amazon KDP		
	Amazon KDP		
	Amazon KDP		
	Amazon KDP		
	Amazon KDP		
	Amazon KDP		
	IngramSpark		
	Draft2Digital / SmashWords		
	Google Play		
	Kobo		
	Nook		

AUG

Date	Income Source	Amount	Total Income
	Apple		
	YouTube		
	Patreon		
	Kickstarter		
		Total Revenue for the month =	

August Expenses

AUG

Find the category that your expense belongs in and drop it in the applicable bucket.
Subtotal at the end of the month and populate the monthly summary

Date	Who did you pay?	Amount
Advertising Expenses: Costs for promoting the business, book promotions, Facebook ads, amazon ads, TikTok ads, website, book launches, etc		
	Total Expense =	

AUG

Date	Who did you pay?	Amount
Commissions: Agent commissions		
	Total Expense =	
Contract Labor: Payments to contractors or freelancers, royalty payments to co-authors or contributors		
	Total Expense =	

AUG

Date	Who did you pay?	Amount
Employee Benefit Programs: costs for employee health insurance		
	Total Expense =	
Insurance: costs of business insurance (not health, dental, home, car, etc)		
	Total Expense =	
Interest: Interest on business loans or credit cards (not your home mortgage interest or student loan interest)		
	Total Expense =	

AUG

Date	Who did you pay?	Amount
Legal and Professional Services: Legal or accounting fees for the business, CPA or tax preparation fees, Payroll processing fees, etc		
	Total Expense =	
Office Expenses: Supplies and expenses related to the business office, Stationery and Supplies, Pens, pencils, notebooks, notepads, paper, envelopes, sticky notes, and other writing materials, Printer and Printer Supplies, Computers, laptops, tablets, Monitors/keyboards/mouses/mousepads, Office Furniture, Any office equipment/furniture that costs less than $2,500, Office Décor, Reference Materials, Author software: Prowriting Aid, Grammarly, World Anvil, Trello, Microsoft, Software subscriptions, shipping, postage,		

AUG

Date	Who did you pay?	Amount
Office Expenses (continued): Supplies and expenses related to the business office, Stationery and Supplies, Pens, pencils, notebooks, notepads, paper, envelopes, sticky notes, and other writing materials, Printer and Printer Supplies, Computers, laptops, tablets, Monitors/keyboards/mouses/ mousepads, Office Furniture, Any office equipment/furniture that costs less than $2,500, Office Décor, Reference Materials, Author software: Prowriting Aid, Grammarly, World Anvil, Trello, Microsoft, Software subscriptions, etc		
	Total Expense =	

AUG

Date	Who did you pay?	Amount
Pension and Profit-Sharing Plans: your business's contributions to employee retirement plans		
	Total Expense =	
Rent: Costs to rent office space, equipment, etc		
	Total Expense =	
Repairs and Maintenance: Costs for repairing or maintaining business property, Laptop repairs, Office furniture repairs		
	Total Expense =	

AUG

Date	Who did you pay?	Amount
Taxes and Licenses: Business-related taxes or licenses, LLC registration, Payroll taxes, Sales taxes, VAT		
	Total Expense =	
Travel: Travel for book signings, author events, or conferences; Registration fees for writing workshops or conferences, Travel for research purposes		
	Total Expense =	
Meals: Business-related meal expenses		
	Total Expense =	

AUG

Date	Who did you pay?	Amount
Utilities: Costs for business utilities if you have an office you rent (electricity, phone, etc.) (not home office utilities)		
	Total Expense =	
Wages: Employee wages or salaries (not your Draw)		
	Total Expense =	
Miscellaneous: Professional development, author classes, etc. (you don't know where to put it, put it here)		
	Total Expense =	

AUG

Date	Who did you pay?	Amount
Book Production Costs: Copyright registration fees, Proofreading and copyediting, Cover designer fees, Book formatting services, ISBN purchases, Printing and distribution costs, Audiobook production fees, Editors, Etc.		
	Total Expense =	

AUG

Here are some extra pages just in case you need more space!

Date	Who did you pay?	Amount	Category

AUG

Here are some extra pages just in case you need more space!

Date	Who did you pay?	Amount	Category

August Home Office

AUG

Date	Who did you pay?	Amount
Electric		
	Total Expense =	
Water/Sewer		
	Total Expense =	
Heating/Oil/Cooling		
	Total Expense =	
Internet/Phone		
	Total Expense =	
Trash/Recycling		
	Total Expense =	

AUG

Date	Who did you pay?	Amount
Home security		
	Total Expense =	
Plowing		
	Total Expense =	
Lawn Maintenance		
	Total Expense =	
Repairs (to home and to office)		
	Total Expense =	
Other		
	Total Expense =	

August Totals

August Home Office Totals

	Amount
Electric	
Water/Sewer	
Heating/Oil/Cooling	
Internet/Phone	
Trash/Recycling	
Home security	
Plowing	
Lawn Maintenance	
Repairs (to home and to office)	
Other	

Add up all of the monthly summary pages to populate the yearly summary sheets

August Income Statement

(Profit & Loss)

	Amount
Total Revenues	
Expenses:	
Advertising	
Car/truck expenses	
Commissions and fees	
Contract labor	
Depreciation	
Employee benefit programs	
Insurance	
Interest	
Legal and Professional	
Office Expense	
Pension/profit-sharing	
Rent/Lease	
Repairs & Maintenance	
Supplies	
Taxes & Licenses	
Travel (not mileage or gas)	
Meals	
Entertainment	
Utilities	
Wages	
Miscellaneous	
Book Production Costs	
Total Expenses	
Net Income (revenue - expenses)	

September Income

SEP

For ease of use, I've populated some common sources of income for you (I hope it helps cut down on your workload!)

Date	Income Source	Amount	Cumulative Total Income
	Amazon KDP		
	Amazon KDP		
	Amazon KDP		
	Amazon KDP		
	Amazon KDP		
	Amazon KDP		
	IngramSpark		
	Draft2Digital / SmashWords		
	Google Play		
	Kobo		
	Nook		

SEP

Date	Income Source	Amount	Total Income
	Apple		
	YouTube		
	Patreon		
	Kickstarter		
		Total Revenue for the month =	

September Expenses

SEP

Find the category that your expense belongs in and drop it in the applicable bucket.
Subtotal at the end of the month and populate the monthly summary

Date	Who did you pay?	Amount
Advertising Expenses: Costs for promoting the business, book promotions, Facebook ads, amazon ads, TikTok ads, website, book launches, etc		
	Total Expense =	

SEP

Date	Who did you pay?	Amount
Commissions: Agent commissions		
	Total Expense =	
Contract Labor: Payments to contractors or freelancers, royalty payments to co-authors or contributors		
	Total Expense =	

SEP

Date	Who did you pay?	Amount
Employee Benefit Programs: costs for employee health insurance		
	Total Expense =	
Insurance: costs of business insurance (<u>not</u> health, dental, home, car, etc)		
	Total Expense =	
Interest: Interest on business loans or credit cards (<u>not</u> your home mortgage interest or student loan interest)		
	Total Expense =	

SEP

Date	Who did you pay?	Amount
Legal and Professional Services: Legal or accounting fees for the business, CPA or tax preparation fees, Payroll processing fees, etc		
	Total Expense =	
Office Expenses: Supplies and expenses related to the business office, Stationery and Supplies, Pens, pencils, notebooks, notepads, paper, envelopes, sticky notes, and other writing materials, Printer and Printer Supplies, Computers, laptops, tablets, Monitors/keyboards/mouses/mousepads, Office Furniture, Any office equipment/furniture that costs less than $2,500, Office Décor, Reference Materials, Author software: Prowriting Aid, Grammarly, World Anvil, Trello, Microsoft, Software subscriptions, shipping, postage.		

SEP

Date	Who did you pay?	Amount
Office Expenses (continued): Supplies and expenses related to the business office, Stationery and Supplies, Pens, pencils, notebooks, notepads, paper, envelopes, sticky notes, and other writing materials, Printer and Printer Supplies, Computers, laptops, tablets, Monitors/keyboards/mouses/ mousepads, Office Furniture, Any office equipment/furniture that costs less than $2,500, Office Décor, Reference Materials, Author software: Prowriting Aid, Grammarly, World Anvil, Trello, Microsoft, Software subscriptions, etc		
	Total Expense =	

SEP

Date	Who did you pay?	Amount
Pension and Profit-Sharing Plans: your business's contributions to employee retirement plans		
	Total Expense =	
Rent: Costs to rent office space, equipment, etc		
	Total Expense =	
Repairs and Maintenance: Costs for repairing or maintaining business property, Laptop repairs, Office furniture repairs		
	Total Expense =	

SEP

Date	Who did you pay?	Amount
Taxes and Licenses: Business-related taxes or licenses, LLC registration, Payroll taxes, Sales taxes, VAT		
	Total Expense =	
Travel: Travel for book signings, author events, or conferences; Registration fees for writing workshops or conferences, Travel for research purposes		
	Total Expense =	
Meals: Business-related meal expenses		
	Total Expense =	

SEP

Date	Who did you pay?	Amount
Utilities: Costs for business utilities if you have an office you rent (electricity, phone, etc.) (not home office utilities)		
	Total Expense =	
Wages: Employee wages or salaries (not your Draw)		
	Total Expense =	
Miscellaneous: Professional development, author classes, etc. (you don't know where to put it, put it here)		
	Total Expense =	

SEP

Date	Who did you pay?	Amount
Book Production Costs: Copyright registration fees, Proofreading and copyediting, Cover designer fees, Book formatting services, ISBN purchases, Printing and distribution costs, Audiobook production fees, Editors, Etc.		
	Total Expense =	

SEP

Here are some extra pages just in case you need more space!

Date	Who did you pay?	Amount	Category

SEP

Here are some extra pages just in case you need more space!

Date	Who did you pay?	Amount	Category

September Home Office

SEP

Date	Who did you pay?	Amount
Electric		
	Total Expense =	
Water/Sewer		
	Total Expense =	
Heating/Oil/Cooling		
	Total Expense =	
Internet/Phone		
	Total Expense =	
Trash/Recycling		
	Total Expense =	

SEP

Date	Who did you pay?	Amount
Home security		
	Total Expense =	
Plowing		
	Total Expense =	
Lawn Maintenance		
	Total Expense =	
Repairs (to home and to office)		
	Total Expense =	
Other		
	Total Expense =	

September Totals

September Home Office Totals

	Amount
Electric	
Water/Sewer	
Heating/Oil/Cooling	
Internet/Phone	
Trash/Recycling	
Home security	
Plowing	
Lawn Maintenance	
Repairs (to home and to office)	
Other	

Add up all of the monthly summary pages to populate the yearly summary sheets

September Income Statement

(Profit & Loss)

	Amount
Total Revenues	
Expenses:	
Advertising	
Car/truck expenses	
Commissions and fees	
Contract labor	
Depreciation	
Employee benefit programs	
Insurance	
Interest	
Legal and Professional	
Office Expense	
Pension/profit-sharing	
Rent/Lease	
Repairs & Maintenance	
Supplies	
Taxes & Licenses	
Travel (not mileage or gas)	
Meals	
Entertainment	
Utilities	
Wages	
Miscellaneous	
Book Production Costs	
Total Expenses	
Net Income (revenue - expenses)	

October Income

OCT

For ease of use, I've populated some common sources of income for you (I hope it helps cut down on your workload!)

Date	Income Source	Amount	Cumulative Total Income
	Amazon KDP		
	Amazon KDP		
	Amazon KDP		
	Amazon KDP		
	Amazon KDP		
	Amazon KDP		
	IngramSpark		
	Draft2Digital / SmashWords		
	Google Play		
	Kobo		
	Nook		

OCT

Date	Income Source	Amount	Total Income
	Apple		
	YouTube		
	Patreon		
	Kickstarter		
		Total Revenue for the month =	

October Expenses

OCT

Find the category that your expense belongs in and drop it in the applicable bucket.
Subtotal at the end of the month and populate the monthly summary

Date	Who did you pay?	Amount
Advertising Expenses: Costs for promoting the business, book promotions, Facebook ads, amazon ads, TikTok ads, website, book launches, etc		
	Total Expense =	

OCT

Date	Who did you pay?	Amount
Commissions: Agent commissions		
	Total Expense =	
Contract Labor: Payments to contractors or freelancers, royalty payments to co-authors or contributors		
	Total Expense =	

OCT

Date	Who did you pay?	Amount
Employee Benefit Programs: costs for employee health insurance		
	Total Expense =	
Insurance: costs of business insurance (not health, dental, home, car, etc)		
	Total Expense =	
Interest: Interest on business loans or credit cards (not your home mortgage interest or student loan interest)		
	Total Expense =	

OCT

Date	Who did you pay?	Amount
Legal and Professional Services: Legal or accounting fees for the business, CPA or tax preparation fees, Payroll processing fees, etc		
	Total Expense =	
Office Expenses: Supplies and expenses related to the business office, Stationery and Supplies, Pens, pencils, notebooks, notepads, paper, envelopes, sticky notes, and other writing materials, Printer and Printer Supplies, Computers, laptops, tablets, Monitors/keyboards/mouses/mousepads, Office Furniture, Any office equipment/furniture that costs less than $2,500, Office Décor, Reference Materials, Author software: Prowriting Aid, Grammarly, World Anvil, Trello, Microsoft, Software subscriptions, shipping, postage.		

OCT

Date	Who did you pay?	Amount
Office Expenses (continued): Supplies and expenses related to the business office, Stationery and Supplies, Pens, pencils, notebooks, notepads, paper, envelopes, sticky notes, and other writing materials, Printer and Printer Supplies, Computers, laptops, tablets, Monitors/keyboards/mouses/ mousepads, Office Furniture, Any office equipment/furniture that costs less than $2,500, Office Décor, Reference Materials, Author software: Prowriting Aid, Grammarly, World Anvil, Trello, Microsoft, Software subscriptions, etc		
	Total Expense =	

OCT

Date	Who did you pay?	Amount
Pension and Profit-Sharing Plans: your business's contributions to employee retirement plans		
	Total Expense =	
Rent: Costs to rent office space, equipment, etc		
	Total Expense =	
Repairs and Maintenance: Costs for repairing or maintaining business property, Laptop repairs, Office furniture repairs		
	Total Expense =	

OCT

Date	Who did you pay?	Amount
Taxes and Licenses: Business-related taxes or licenses, LLC registration, Payroll taxes, Sales taxes, VAT		
	Total Expense =	
Travel: Travel for book signings, author events, or conferences; Registration fees for writing workshops or conferences, Travel for research purposes		
	Total Expense =	
Meals: Business-related meal expenses		
	Total Expense =	

OCT

Date	Who did you pay?	Amount
Utilities: Costs for business utilities if you have an office you rent (electricity, phone, etc.) (not home office utilities)		
	Total Expense =	
Wages: Employee wages or salaries (not your Draw)		
	Total Expense =	
Miscellaneous: Professional development, author classes, etc. (you don't know where to put it, put it here)		
	Total Expense =	

OCT

Date	Who did you pay?	Amount
Book Production Costs: Copyright registration fees, Proofreading and copyediting, Cover designer fees, Book formatting services, ISBN purchases, Printing and distribution costs, Audiobook production fees, Editors, Etc.		
	Total Expense =	

OCT

Here are some extra pages just in case you need more space!

Date	Who did you pay?	Amount	Category

OCT

Here are some extra pages just in case you need more space!

Date	Who did you pay?	Amount	Category

October Home Office

OCT

Date	Who did you pay?	Amount
Electric		
	Total Expense =	
Water/Sewer		
	Total Expense =	
Heating/Oil/Cooling		
	Total Expense =	
Internet/Phone		
	Total Expense =	
Trash/Recycling		
	Total Expense =	

OCT

Date	Who did you pay?	Amount
Home security		
	Total Expense =	
Plowing		
	Total Expense =	
Lawn Maintenance		
	Total Expense =	
Repairs (to home and to office)		
	Total Expense =	
Other		
	Total Expense =	

October Totals

October Home Office Totals

	Amount
Electric	
Water/Sewer	
Heating/Oil/Cooling	
Internet/Phone	
Trash/Recycling	
Home security	
Plowing	
Lawn Maintenance	
Repairs (to home and to office)	
Other	

Add up all of the monthly summary pages to populate the yearly summary sheets

October Income Statement

(Profit & Loss)

	Amount
Total Revenues	
Expenses:	
Advertising	
Car/truck expenses	
Commissions and fees	
Contract labor	
Depreciation	
Employee benefit programs	
Insurance	
Interest	
Legal and Professional	
Office Expense	
Pension/profit-sharing	
Rent/Lease	
Repairs & Maintenance	
Supplies	
Taxes & Licenses	
Travel (not mileage or gas)	
Meals	
Entertainment	
Utilities	
Wages	
Miscellaneous	
Book Production Costs	
Total Expenses	
Net Income (revenue - expenses)	

November Income

NOV

For ease of use, I've populated some common sources of income for you (I hope it helps cut down on your workload!)

Date	Income Source	Amount	Cumulative Total Income
	Amazon KDP		
	Amazon KDP		
	Amazon KDP		
	Amazon KDP		
	Amazon KDP		
	Amazon KDP		
	IngramSpark		
	Draft2Digital / SmashWords		
	Google Play		
	Kobo		
	Nook		

NOV

Date	Income Source	Amount	Total Income
	Apple		
	YouTube		
	Patreon		
	Kickstarter		
		Total Revenue for the month =	

November Expenses

NOV

Find the category that your expense belongs in and drop it in the applicable bucket.
Subtotal at the end of the month and populate the monthly summary

Date	Who did you pay?	Amount
Advertising Expenses: Costs for promoting the business, book promotions, Facebook ads, amazon ads, TikTok ads, website, book launches, etc		
	Total Expense =	

NOV

Date	Who did you pay?	Amount
Commissions: Agent commissions		
	Total Expense =	
Contract Labor: Payments to contractors or freelancers, royalty payments to co-authors or contributors		
	Total Expense =	

NOV

Date	Who did you pay?	Amount
Employee Benefit Programs: costs for employee health insurance		
	Total Expense =	
Insurance: costs of business insurance (not health, dental, home, car, etc)		
	Total Expense =	
Interest: Interest on business loans or credit cards (not your home mortgage interest or student loan interest)		
	Total Expense =	

NOV

Date	Who did you pay?	Amount
Legal and Professional Services: Legal or accounting fees for the business, CPA or tax preparation fees, Payroll processing fees, etc		
	Total Expense =	
Office Expenses: Supplies and expenses related to the business office, Stationery and Supplies, Pens, pencils, notebooks, notepads, paper, envelopes, sticky notes, and other writing materials, Printer and Printer Supplies, Computers, laptops, tablets, Monitors/keyboards/mouses/mousepads, Office Furniture, Any office equipment/furniture that costs less than $2,500, Office Décor, Reference Materials, Author software: Prowriting Aid, Grammarly, World Anvil, Trello, Microsoft, Software subscriptions, shipping, postage,		

NOV

Date	Who did you pay?	Amount
Office Expenses (continued): Supplies and expenses related to the business office, Stationery and Supplies, Pens, pencils, notebooks, notepads, paper, envelopes, sticky notes, and other writing materials, Printer and Printer Supplies, Computers, laptops, tablets, Monitors/keyboards/mouses/ mousepads, Office Furniture, Any office equipment/furniture that costs less than $2,500, Office Décor, Reference Materials, Author software: Prowriting Aid, Grammarly, World Anvil, Trello, Microsoft, Software subscriptions, etc		
	Total Expense =	

NOV

Date	Who did you pay?	Amount
Pension and Profit-Sharing Plans: your business's contributions to employee retirement plans		
	Total Expense =	
Rent: Costs to rent office space, equipment, etc		
	Total Expense =	
Repairs and Maintenance: Costs for repairing or maintaining business property, Laptop repairs, Office furniture repairs		
	Total Expense =	

NOV

Date	Who did you pay?	Amount
Taxes and Licenses: Business-related taxes or licenses, LLC registration, Payroll taxes, Sales taxes, VAT		
	Total Expense =	
Travel: Travel for book signings, author events, or conferences; Registration fees for writing workshops or conferences, Travel for research purposes		
	Total Expense =	
Meals: Business-related meal expenses		
	Total Expense =	

NOV

Date	Who did you pay?	Amount
Utilities: Costs for business utilities if you have an office you rent (electricity, phone, etc.) (not home office utilities)		
	Total Expense =	
Wages: Employee wages or salaries (not your Draw)		
	Total Expense =	
Miscellaneous: Professional development, author classes, etc. (you don't know where to put it, put it here)		
	Total Expense =	

NOV

Date	Who did you pay?	Amount
Book Production Costs: Copyright registration fees, Proofreading and copyediting, Cover designer fees, Book formatting services, ISBN purchases, Printing and distribution costs, Audiobook production fees, Editors, Etc.		
	Total Expense =	

NOV

Here are some extra pages just in case you need more space!

Date	Who did you pay?	Amount	Category

NOV

Here are some extra pages just in case you need more space!

Date	Who did you pay?	Amount	Category

November Home Office

NOV

Date	Who did you pay?	Amount
Electric		
	Total Expense =	
Water/Sewer		
	Total Expense =	
Heating/Oil/Cooling		
	Total Expense =	
Internet/Phone		
	Total Expense =	
Trash/Recycling		
	Total Expense =	

NOV

Date	Who did you pay?	Amount
Home security		
	Total Expense =	
Plowing		
	Total Expense =	
Lawn Maintenance		
	Total Expense =	
Repairs (to home and to office)		
	Total Expense =	
Other		
	Total Expense =	

November Totals

November Home Office Totals

	Amount
Electric	
Water/Sewer	
Heating/Oil/Cooling	
Internet/Phone	
Trash/Recycling	
Home security	
Plowing	
Lawn Maintenance	
Repairs (to home and to office)	
Other	

Add up all of the monthly summary pages to populate the yearly summary sheets

November Income Statement

(Profit & Loss)

	Amount
Total Revenues	
Expenses:	
Advertising	
Car/truck expenses	
Commissions and fees	
Contract labor	
Depreciation	
Employee benefit programs	
Insurance	
Interest	
Legal and Professional	
Office Expense	
Pension/profit-sharing	
Rent/Lease	
Repairs & Maintenance	
Supplies	
Taxes & Licenses	
Travel (not mileage or gas)	
Meals	
Entertainment	
Utilities	
Wages	
Miscellaneous	
Book Production Costs	
Total Expenses	
Net Income (revenue - expenses)	

December Income

DEC

For ease of use, I've populated some common sources of income for you (I hope it helps cut down on your workload!)

Date	Income Source	Amount	Cumulative Total Income
	Amazon KDP		
	Amazon KDP		
	Amazon KDP		
	Amazon KDP		
	Amazon KDP		
	Amazon KDP		
	IngramSpark		
	Draft2Digital / SmashWords		
	Google Play		
	Kobo		
	Nook		

DEC

Date	Income Source	Amount	Total Income
	Apple		
	YouTube		
	Patreon		
	Kickstarter		
		Total Revenue for the month =	

December Expenses

DEC

Find the category that your expense belongs in and drop it in the applicable bucket.
Subtotal at the end of the month and populate the monthly summary

Date	Who did you pay?	Amount
Advertising Expenses: Costs for promoting the business, book promotions, Facebook ads, amazon ads, TikTok ads, website, book launches, etc		
	Total Expense =	

DEC

Date	Who did you pay?	Amount
Commissions: Agent commissions		
	Total Expense =	
Contract Labor: Payments to contractors or freelancers, royalty payments to co-authors or contributors		
	Total Expense =	

DEC

Date	Who did you pay?	Amount
Employee Benefit Programs: costs for employee health insurance		
	Total Expense =	
Insurance: costs of business insurance (<u>not</u> health, dental, home, car, etc)		
	Total Expense =	
Interest: Interest on business loans or credit cards (<u>not</u> your home mortgage interest or student loan interest)		
	Total Expense =	

DEC

Date	Who did you pay?	Amount
Legal and Professional Services: Legal or accounting fees for the business, CPA or tax preparation fees, Payroll processing fees, etc		
	Total Expense =	
Office Expenses: Supplies and expenses related to the business office, Stationery and Supplies, Pens, pencils, notebooks, notepads, paper, envelopes, sticky notes, and other writing materials, Printer and Printer Supplies, Computers, laptops, tablets, Monitors/keyboards/mouses/mousepads, Office Furniture, Any office equipment/furniture that costs less than $2,500, Office Décor, Reference Materials, Author software: Prowriting Aid, Grammarly, World Anvil, Trello, Microsoft, Software subscriptions, shipping, postage,		

DEC

Date	Who did you pay?	Amount
Office Expenses (continued): Supplies and expenses related to the business office, Stationery and Supplies, Pens, pencils, notebooks, notepads, paper, envelopes, sticky notes, and other writing materials, Printer and Printer Supplies, Computers, laptops, tablets, Monitors/keyboards/mouses/ mousepads, Office Furniture, Any office equipment/furniture that costs less than $2,500, Office Décor, Reference Materials, Author software: Prowriting Aid, Grammarly, World Anvil, Trello, Microsoft, Software subscriptions, etc		
	Total Expense =	

DEC

Date	Who did you pay?	Amount
Pension and Profit-Sharing Plans: your business's contributions to employee retirement plans		
	Total Expense =	
Rent: Costs to rent office space, equipment, etc		
	Total Expense =	
Repairs and Maintenance: Costs for repairing or maintaining business property, Laptop repairs, Office furniture repairs		
	Total Expense =	

DEC

Date	Who did you pay?	Amount
Taxes and Licenses: Business-related taxes or licenses, LLC registration, Payroll taxes, Sales taxes, VAT		
	Total Expense =	
Travel: Travel for book signings, author events, or conferences; Registration fees for writing workshops or conferences, Travel for research purposes		
	Total Expense =	
Meals: Business-related meal expenses		
	Total Expense =	

DEC

Date	Who did you pay?	Amount
Utilities: Costs for business utilities if you have an office you rent (electricity, phone, etc.) (not home office utilities)		
	Total Expense =	
Wages: Employee wages or salaries (not your Draw)		
	Total Expense =	
Miscellaneous: Professional development, author classes, etc. (you don't know where to put it, put it here)		
	Total Expense =	

DEC

Date	Who did you pay?	Amount
Book Production Costs: Copyright registration fees, Proofreading and copyediting, Cover designer fees, Book formatting services, ISBN purchases, Printing and distribution costs, Audiobook production fees, Editors, Etc.		
	Total Expense =	

DEC

Here are some extra pages just in case you need more space!

Date	Who did you pay?	Amount	Category

DEC

Here are some extra pages just in case you need more space!

Date	Who did you pay?	Amount	Category

December Home Office

DEC

Date	Who did you pay?	Amount
Electric		
	Total Expense =	
Water/Sewer		
	Total Expense =	
Heating/Oil/Cooling		
	Total Expense =	
Internet/Phone		
	Total Expense =	
Trash/Recycling		
	Total Expense =	

DEC

Date	Who did you pay?	Amount
Home security		
	Total Expense =	
Plowing		
	Total Expense =	
Lawn Maintenance		
	Total Expense =	
Repairs (to home and to office)		
	Total Expense =	
Other		
	Total Expense =	

December Totals

December Home Office Totals

	Amount
Electric	
Water/Sewer	
Heating/Oil/Cooling	
Internet/Phone	
Trash/Recycling	
Home security	
Plowing	
Lawn Maintenance	
Repairs (to home and to office)	
Other	

Add up all of the monthly summary pages to populate the yearly summary sheets

December Income Statement

(Profit & Loss)

	Amount
Total Revenues	
Expenses:	
Advertising	
Car/truck expenses	
Commissions and fees	
Contract labor	
Depreciation	
Employee benefit programs	
Insurance	
Interest	
Legal and Professional	
Office Expense	
Pension/profit-sharing	
Rent/Lease	
Repairs & Maintenance	
Supplies	
Taxes & Licenses	
Travel (not mileage or gas)	
Meals	
Entertainment	
Utilities	
Wages	
Miscellaneous	
Book Production Costs	
Total Expenses	
Net Income (revenue - expenses)	

Yearly Income Statement (Profit & Loss)

You will populate this schedule with the combined totals from your monthly summaries and the final result will be the numbers for your tax return

Income Statement (Profit & Loss)

	Amount
Total Revenues	
Expenses:	
Advertising	
Car/truck expenses	
Commissions and fees	
Contract labor	
Depreciation	
Employee benefit programs	
Insurance	
Interest	
Legal and Professional	
Office Expense	
Pension/profit-sharing	
Rent/Lease	
Repairs & Maintenance	
Supplies	
Taxes & Licenses	
Travel (not mileage or gas)	
Meals	
Entertainment	
Utilities	
Wages	
Miscellaneous	
Book Production Costs	
Total Expenses	
Net Income (revenue - expenses)	

Give to your tax preparer

Home Office Totals

Drop your yearly totals for all of your home office expenses here. This is what you can take a copy of and **give to your tax preparer**

Total square footage of your office - ____________

Total square footage of your home - ____________

Sq ft of office / sq. ft of home = percent you can potentially deduct - __________%

Expense	Total amount for the year
Mortgage Interest (from 1009 - you don't need to copy it here but you can if you want)	
Property Taxes (from 1009 - you don't need to copy it here but you can if you want)	
Electric	
Water & Sewer	
Heating/Cooling/Oil	
Internet/Phone	
Trash/Recycling	
Home Security	
Plowing	
Lawn Maintenance	
Repairs	
Other	

That's it. Easy peasy.

That's basically your Schedule C tax return!

Either give a copy of this page to your preparer or use it to enter the info yourself

Congrats on keeping such beautiful records!

An Easier Way

- It can get cumbersome to do paper record-keeping, especially as your business begins to scale.
- Personally, I'm a computer-person, therefore I love digitalizing my record-keeping. I'm even able to make my excel trackers as pretty as this workbook.
- **I created an incredible Excel workbook that I have available for sale that can do the math for you, if that's something you're interested in going forward.**
    - Don't worry if your computer skills are incredible - this file is bomb-proof. You won't be able to mess it up (unless you really try to)

- Also, if it gets to the point where you just don't want to worry about the record-keeping anymore, I'm currently a huge fan of QuickBooks Online. **I can basically set it up so it mostly automates the bookkeeping.** I link my bank and credit card feeds to it, set up some accounting rules, and most of my transactions are recorded for me.
    - I like information so I also select book/series/pen name to track profitability for each segment of my business so that takes a little extra time but I love the automation.
    - **It's really amazing being able to look at each segment of your business and at a glance determine profitability so you can double-down or abandon a project (then again, I'm a CPA and I love the freedom of knowledge)**
    - That's my long way of saying that if you want something a little more robust than an excel tracker (or this awesome organizer) then I can help you
    - It automates so much for me (after I took the time to set it up) that **I only spend a few minutes on my bookkeeping every month.**
- If either of these offerings sound good…reach out. I'd love to help transform your finances!

Month-end & Year-end Checklists

Month-end Checklist

Use this on a monthly basis to stay on top of your to-do list

- Review Income and Expenses:
  - **Categorize income and expenses** accurately.
- Bank Reconciliation:
  - Reconcile bank statements with accounting records to ensure accuracy and detect any discrepancies.
  - **Tip: if you don't already have a separate checking account for your business - please, please, please consider doing so. Please. (Did I make it clear how important this is?)**
  - Also, if you use a payment processor (e.g. - PayPal), try to **have a different one for business and personal transactions.**
    - Do your best to **keep business funds separate from personal funds.**
      - Look up "piercing the corporate veil"
- Tax Preparations:
  - Take a look at any tax obligations for the month
    - Any quarterly estimates owed?
    - Any Sales tax owed?
    - Any Payroll taxes owed?
    - Double check any payroll tax withholdings have all gone through the filing system and were accepted

Month-end Checklist

- Review Cash Flow:
    - Analyze cash flow for the month to understand income and expense patterns.
- Document Management:
    - Keep records organized for tax reporting purposes, ensuring all necessary documents are in order.
- Evaluate Marketing Efforts:
    - Review the effectiveness of marketing strategies or promotional efforts carried out during the month.
- **Backup Data:**
    - Backup digital financial records
    - Backup any writing drafts/notes
- Plan for the Next Month and Review Prior Month
    - Review goals, set goals, plan projects, or outline tasks for the upcoming month to maintain productivity.

Year-end Checklist

Use this to make sure you have everything ready for tax prep to ensure a smooth, stress-free process

- Were you required to file 1099's? If yes, did you?
    - Tip - 1099s are required to any person you paid more than $600 to during the year who is not an S or C Corp ($10+ for royalties)
        - LLC doesn't *not* stand for limited liability *corporation*
    - Ask vendors for a completed W9 as backup
    - If you paid someone via PayPal/Venmo/square/etc. *business* then you may not need to issue 1099s to them (unless you paid them via 'friends and family' - then they might need one)
- Mileage driven for work and total milage driven (you need to provide both)
    - **Included in this workbook**
- Home office questions: Square footage of your home office, square footage of your home, total paid for home's: mortgage interest, property taxes, insurance, repairs/maintenance, snow plowing, internet, electric, oil, water/sewer, etc
    - **Included in this workbook**
- Did you have any sales that are reportable to other states?
    - If yes, how much and where?
- Income Statement (aka Profit & Loss)
    - **Included in this workbook**

Year-end Checklist

- Any payroll returns/forms
- If you are anything other than a schedule C filer, you'll also need to give balance sheet items
    - Bank/cash balance, loan balances, what you took out/put in, etc
- Did you buy anything over $2,500 during the year?
    - If so, what was it?
- Did you make any federal or state estimates?
    - If so, list amounts and dates
- Did you contribute to your self employed retirement plan?
    - If so, how much?
    - Would you want to contribute the max amount?
- Did you reconcile your bank statements?
- Did you remember to include the expenses that were on your credit card at 12/31 but you hadn't paid off yet?
    - You still get to deduct those - even if it was charged and not paid yet

What else do I offer?

- **I offer trainings in Excel / QuickBooks Online**
  - I can custom set-up your QBO account, including the-set up of bank feeds to <u>automate</u> your bookkeeping as much as possible. Your time is valuable. Spend it writing rather than record-keeping. Leave the bookkeeping to the software
  - I also have an Excel tracking spreadsheet to streamline foolproof record keeping for the number-nervous author. It doesn't offer the same automation but it's easier than this paper organizer in the sense that it does math for you

- I've created *this* **Bookkeeping Organizer for Authors** workbook
  - *Thanks for buying!*

- I've created an **Author's Business and Financial Handbook: Tips for Bookkeeping, Accounting, and Taxes**

- But….if you're here and still reading this, then **PLEASE take a few minutes and leave a review on Amazon**. As an author, you know how amazing that is, and I'd really appreciate any feedback on this journal so I can keep improving it :-)